Notes from Heaven

Robert Frandeen

Garden Light Productions
Sarasota, Florida

Dedication

Thank you, Robyn, for always believing.

NOTES FROM HEAVEN
Robert Frandeen

A Garden Light Productions book published in arrangement with the author.
Published by Garden Light Productions, Sarasota, FL

Library of Congress Control Number: 2013950531

ISBN: 978-0-9899738-1-6

During a trip to Paris in September, 2005, I took a number of pictures of the Circle of Twelve Angels by Jean Jacques Pradier in the crypt of Les Invalides in Paris. At the time I was moved by the force of presence and beauty of the twelve stone angels, but time was scarce and I quickly moved on to the rest of Paris. I did not give the angels much further thought.

Some weeks later, at home in Santa Cruz, California, as I was looking at the prints of the angels, I heard a ringing in my ears and a voice calling my name. She spoke in a comforting and compelling way. She said she was an Angel of Heaven. I wrote down what she said to me over a period of several days.

Robert Frandeen
February 28, 2006
Santa Cruz, California

I

I feel inadequate describing Heaven to you because I have not been here long as these things are measured, and my understanding is constantly expanding. By comparison to those around me, I have little knowledge or experience on this side. However, it is because I am not so far removed from your side that I am better able to convey to you the sense of what Heaven is like. Those on this side for the most part no longer know language. Communication is on a different level of perception that does not translate easily. I will do my best for you. I will try and explain to you what I do here and, more importantly, what all of Heaven works at, and I do mean work. It is not eternal bliss. There is a celebration upon arrival by all who know you, but then it is back to work. We all have our work, though that word or thought is not used here. It is simply what you do once you are here. I will give you my present understanding of what I do, though there are many other things to do here that I know nothing about.

As is often the case, I arrived here in the company of many others. There was a crowd to greet us. Our entire families were here and many others who had known us during our lives and were simply happy for our arrival. The number of people who follow your every thought and move on the Earth is awesome and, of course, when you first come over and see for yourself, it is quite a grand surprise which can seem to go on forever, but at the end there is work to do. People who love you and greet you go off to do what they do here, and you are left with your first instructions for what you will do here. Everyone eventually receives their first instructions in Heaven, and you wear them openly on a long translucent sash of intricate colors. It is your first real sign of being here, a true citizen of Heaven.

Your first instructions are not forced upon you, and sometimes there is much you need to do for yourself before you receive your first instructions, so they are left for you to seek them when you are ready. When I did finally go for my instructions, it was to a small building in the center of a large city that housed a library of events that had happened in time, a place where I had spent much of my "time" since my arrival. I met with the librarian there, a very wise and wonderful woman, and she told me to go to a place near the Light of Creation. Somehow, I knew where that was.

The Light of Creation is blinding to see at first, even from a distance. I first saw it as a distant line of brightness on the far horizon of Heaven. The librarian told me to go in that direction and that I would meet the one who would instruct me. She placed in my hand what looked like a red jewel, and as I thought about going in that direction, I literally began to fly there. It was a very far journey even as these things are measured in Heaven. Flying itself is so wonderful and the sights so glorious, it was easy to forget where I was going and just succumb to the joy of soaring.

Whatever you think occurs as you fly across Heaven: up, down, over, faster, slower, stop, swoop. You are like the finest most sensitive flying machine, only it is your own body over which you have absolute confidence and control, a body of comfort, no sense of wind, heat, cold, only the sheer joy of soaring over all of Heaven. Even now, I still do it. I love to fly just for the wonder and joy of it and the never ending heavenly sights.

After what seemed forever, I was still far from what was now an enormous wall of light against the horizon, light so bright I dared not look. The blinding wall of light was still infinitely far away even though I had crossed all of Heaven, and I was wondering if my journey would be an eternal one when I saw where I was going. Sitting at the base of a hill crowned with golden flowers was a house of white stone next to a pool of clear water. There were several people standing by the pool talking to a woman with long, silver hair and eyes that sparkled with the same light as the wall of light in the far distance. She turned and smiled at me and opened her arms to me, and I wept and fell down and had to be helped up.

She embraced me in her loving arms and spoke to me in a voice I had always known but never heard. She instructed me there at that white stone house next to that pool of clear water, myself and many others who came and went, some to be instructed, some seeking wisdom, some to just be with her. She is there still, still instructing and sharing her wisdom with all who need it and come to her. She spoke her name to me, but I cannot repeat it here, not because it is forbidden, but because there is simply no sound or word that can express it. It seemed a lifetime later, she took both my hands in hers and she took me to the wall of light that is the Light of Creation, and she instructed me in what I must do there.

II

The Light of Creation can best be expressed as a wall of light when you see it from afar, but up close you can see that coming out of the brightness that seems to stretch in every direction forever, is a full image record in vivid colors of all that has ever taken place in the heart of creation. Every word uttered and every moment breathed in every life lived is recorded in a perfect and exact brilliant color record that flows eternally out of the Light of Creation. In Heaven, this perfect record of interwoven lives is called the Tapestry of Life. Every human life is recorded in the Tapestry of Life as a single thread of many colors, and all the threads are interwoven into unimaginably beautiful and intricate patterns of life, each more awe inspiring than the last.

The great beauty of the Tapestry of Life from a distance is something all in Heaven come often to see. It is one of the greater attractions in Heaven. Each soul can point to a part they played in the Fabric of Life, a lifeline of beautiful colors with a myriad of connections to other lives and lines of complementing colors. Every life counts equally in the fabrication of the Tapestry of Life, for the Tapestry of Life is a whole cloth beyond perfection where there are no missing stitches, no incomplete patterns. Some threads are more delicate than others, and some shine and are infinitely beautiful with purples and golds and colors never seen before. Some life threads are solid and bold and strong and hold whole sections together. All of the life threads are part of one connecting pattern or another. No life thread is left alone and isolated, unconnected to the surrounding pattern. The Sacred Books of Heaven say that at the End of Time all of Heaven will gather and witness God to appear before us wrapped in the Fabric of Life as a heavenly garment. We will not see God, but we will see the beauty and shape of God, as God honors all of Creation by donning before us with great pride the garment that was made with our very lives.

The other side of the Light of Creation is seldom seen by those in

Heaven. My Instructor has brought us there many times, and she has pointed out important events certain to come in Creation, but we do not go there regularly. Only the Council of the Wise in Heaven travel there regularly to examine the other side of the Light of Creation for trends and possibilities in Creation in order to give wisdom about present problems. Their findings and motives are not regularly revealed to us in Heaven, and though my Instructor goes often to the Council of the Wise in Heaven to receive her instructions, she does not discuss with us what takes place. I have never been to the Council of the Wise in Heaven, and in telling you these things, there is much I do not know or understand. The other side of the Light of Creation is one, but I will do my best to say what I know.

Projecting out in front of the opposite side of the wall of light that is the Light of Creation is a shifting glow of things to come as far as the eye can see. Some clear outlines in solid colors can be seen, but with shifting borders and patterns inside those outlines, and still more vague shapes as you try to look closer at groups and individual lives inside those patterns. The moment you look away and then look back, those patterns and colors have changed and they continue to change until the final moment when they are sealed for all eternity into the final Fabric of Life that flows eternally out the other side.

Lines and colors constantly shift on the future side of the Light of Creation, and it can be difficult to understand any of what you are seeing, and few from Heaven ever venture there. Such is the future of Creation — shifting uncertainty. There is no more certainty in Heaven about the final outcome of

Creation than there is on Earth, but there is a much higher knowledge and faith in God's ultimate purpose in Creation. Nothing but the highest beauty has ever flowed out of the Light of Creation, no matter what the future possibilities, and it is for this purpose of keeping the flow of beauty that we do our work. Only a select few can enter into the center of the Light of Creation, and only those with our purpose. All of Heaven watches the outcome, but few know the intimate present. My Instructor is a master of the present in the very center of the Light of Creation and this is where I work, seeking to accomplish as she instructs me. I am a small part of an enormous work that is on-going in every decision of every moment of every life in Creation. It is a work concerned with achieving the highest level of beauty from every individual effort in every moment of Creation and recording that moment for all eternity.

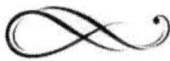

III

During instructions our Instructor speaks to us in long sessions in her white stone house of seemingly infinite rooms and colors. Outside, her house looks modest, but inside there are great halls and winding staircases. We often sit at long comfortable tables in enormous rooms with live music and open ceilings to ever changing skies. She will talk to us at length about our work in the Light of Creation. We walk with her in her lush gardens behind the house, and we visit her stables and many horses as she instructs us. We often gather around her in the quiet of the evening by the pool of clear water. Her eyes will glow bright as she raises her beautiful hands in a graceful movement and the pool of clear water will light with golden colors.

As our Instructor slowly moves her hands, scenes appear in the pool of golden light, and she will explain to us the meaning of the scenes, and then she will tell us what is needed and possible in order for the best to come of the situation. She moves her hands high over her head, and the pool will glow into a fainter silvery light with many shadows, and then she will show us all the possible futures to come for that situation, and she will discuss with us with great love and affection what we must seek to accomplish by influencing a certain present moment. Once we all understand all that she has said, we join hands with our Instructor and appear in the present moment in which all decisions are locked into place forever.

The individuals we come to visit in the present moment cannot see us, but our visits are carefully chosen to be with those individuals in those times and places where those we visit are in the most probable condition to hear and feel what we are saying and to act on it. Relatively few individuals at any one time on the Earth are ever in a condition to hear us and fewer still will act, but there are always more than enough to keep us all eternally busy. Our job is simple, yet so important. We hold the thoughts we wish the individual to hear, and these thoughts are only and always of one nature - they are always of God's nature. The thoughts we hold are always the invisible attributes of

God's nature. God is mercy by definition, and this is most often the thought we hold in our minds as we stand in the moment, only this invisible but powerful thought of mercy until that thought is felt and acted upon, and the change we came to achieve has begun.

There are many other thoughts and combination of thoughts that we invade a present moment with, but they are always the attributes of God: Love, Mercy, Wisdom, Beauty, these are the most common thoughts we hold in the moment. Once acted upon, we can see the colors of a situation begin to change before our eyes, and our job will be done. Few on Earth ever see the change. The action taken can seem quite miniscule. Never are we involved with major decisions. The big decisions in life for the most part are already made. It is only the small acts of forgiveness and kindness that we come to insert in the present moment, and we can only do so because a certain individual at a certain moment in time is willing to open up to us. These small acts of kindness and mercy are like small seeds. They grow and prosper many times over many generations. Even though this might not be visible at the time, the beauty in the end will be quite clear. After each event, we gather again at the white house of our Instructor and she leads us in a prayer of thanksgiving. We then view the results in the pool of bright water and there is great celebration and joy; and then she shows us in her pool of bright water what next must be done.

Our Instructor is one of many, and she receives her instructions in ways that I am not certain. There are many pools of clear water such as ours with similar missions to our own. Our

Instructor often goes to meet with other Instructors, and sometimes she goes to the Council of the Wise in Heaven. I do not know how the moments she is given are selected, but I know that the moments are selected and coordinated all across the same moment of time in the very center of the Light of Creation by the Council of the Wise in Heaven. The Council of the Wise in Heaven consults on the far side of the Light of Creation, and they then look into the very heart of each moment in time to see best what can be done in order to seal into place the most perfect moment.

Then the Instructors are called and sent on their missions.

I cannot see the wide picture stretched over all of time in my limited vision. I can barely see events as our Instructor explains them to me in her pool of bright water, and I can focus only on my limited tasks at hand. But I know that at the same moment I am doing my task, thousands of others like me are doing the same thing. We are infusing that particular moment in time with God's attributes, and significant choices are made in that moment and reverberate down through all of time.

You were present at one of our moments in time. The individual we were seeking to influence sat a table away from you. We noticed that you stopped reading the book you were reading and began to write down our thoughts. I had heard of this happening before, but I had never seen it happen. Later when we reviewed what had happened at the pool of bright water, it was decided that we would see what else you could write. I was chosen for this for the reasons I have explained. I am standing here now as you write these words.

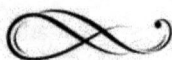

IV

A large part of our instruction is about color. Everything has color, infinite color, shades and variations, and infinite possibilities of matching colors. When I see you on the Earth in this moment we are now sitting in, the colors I see are not what you see. I see the emotions and thought patterns of you and those around you, not as words and ideas, but as colors and patterns, and it is the colors I place most meaning on.

The words I am choosing for you are difficult in that I am seeking the correct colors in the words I choose. This is why it is difficult to translate. Colors tell at a glance what is going on in any given situation on Earth or in Heaven. There is no need to ask for thoughts and opinions. The colors tell. I do not know what you are thinking because I can read the words of your mind. I know what you are thinking because I can read the colors that are emanating from you, so can anyone else. There are no secrets in Heaven or on Earth.

We study in our instruction the combinations and subtleties of colors and patterns throughout the entirety of the Light of Creation, which as far as anyone can tell, has no end. The final outcome of everything in Creation is always color, color so brilliant and astonishing, that all of Heaven comes regularly to marvel at the on going Tapestry of Life. Once is not enough, especially when everyone realizes what an important and truly colorful life they lived and contributed. When you come to Heaven, you, too, will come to marvel more than once. No life is without astonishingly brilliant color. It is why the Light of Creation shines so brightly in Heaven. All the individual lives on Earth together give off a light so bright it cannot be looked at from Heaven. No one life is any less brilliant than the next no matter what the color. It is the individual soul that supplies the individual lights that together form one magnificently brilliant heavenly light. It is each uniquely colorful individual life that gives the astonishing variety of colors in overall patterns. All souls shine equal, and each life has unique color.

It is color we come to influence on Earth. We do this with the unique color of God's attributes that we emanate. When we think of God's attributes, a certain color permeates the psychic atmosphere. We are seeking to literally swamp the brain waves of the persons we are seeking to influence. There is still choice. We still can only create atmosphere. But God's attributes are powerful, and we seldom fail, and even then, there is some benefit. We can see colors change before our eyes, long before the individual is aware of a new thought pattern. As thought inside the individual begins to take hold, new colors begin to emanate, colors never seen before. If you were able to ask the individual if anything had taken place, they would probably say no. Certainly, to anyone around, nothing happened. But the color tells. And we can follow the color down through time. The color always tells the story, and the story is about Beauty, not ordinary beauty, but God's Beauty. Beauty is an attribute of God. God is Beauty – and all of Creation is measured by that standard of beauty. The goal of our work on the Tapestry of Life is to make it the most beautiful it can be as measured against God's Beauty. The way this is done is by infusing the Tapestry of Life with the most reflections of God's attributes as is Heavenly possible. The only way this can happen is by having the most individual soul lights as is Heavenly possible give off the unique colors of God's attributes all down through the march of time. It is these individual and uniquely astounding colors of brilliance that all of Heaven comes so often to see in the Tapestry of Life. Every time one of God's attributes is embraced in a life an unbelievable color of light happens and this light is embedded forever in the Tapestry of Life. When we get to see this happen before our eyes when we gather with our Instructor in the cool of the evening and look into her pool of bright water, there is exhilaration I cannot convey. It is why we do what we do.

∞

V

Wisdom is golden, and it is the most prominent color our Instructor emanates. When someone speaks in Heaven, their personal colors beam out in an array of colors behind them that tells the emotions and motives of what is meant before anything has been spoken. There is speaking in Heaven. Words are precious and chosen with care, and their spoken sounds come in the form of music. The sound of our Instructor's voice, together with the colors she emanates is transfixing. The room swells with color and sound. Often, she has accompaniment when she instructs. Great musicians from all over Heaven come to hear her voice and play beside her. As she speaks, they close their eyes and play. The golden glow of her spoken wisdom and the sound her voice makes together with the musicians around her is something only Heaven can know, and it is what makes our ability to do this great work with her one of Heaven's highest blessings. Wisdom is most prized in Heaven, much the way gold is on Earth, and people come from all over Heaven to see her golden aura and hear her song of wisdom. Being able to sit at the same table as our Instructor while these things are taking place is an honor I can never express in words. Our instruction with her is seldom in closed sessions. Many in Heaven stop what they are doing to come and hear her words. It is most difficult to sit with her and not swell with pride that we can be there sitting at her table. Of course, she can see this. There is great merriment at these sessions. Love and affection, too, are most prominent with her.

The color of wisdom is the most difficult of all the colors in Heaven to wear, and it is the most precious. I have never been on a trip into the Light of Creation to hold and carry the color of wisdom. Others much more accomplished than I go with our Instructor. Missions of wisdom are important, but seldom. Few on Earth can hear true wisdom. I have sometimes been able to show sparks of wisdom during my instruction, but not consistently, not to hold in place as we travel from Heaven to Earth. I pursue my individual studies when these trips are done.

Personal wisdom is a large part of my instruction and much of this instruction occurs in the library of my Instructor's white stone house. On close inspection, the white stones are a crush of translucent gem like material that can change shape at any time and glow with all the colors of Heaven. The library is larger than the largest library on Earth. There is even a private librarian and assistants too numerous to count. A woman of astonishing beauty sits at a wide marble table in the very front of the library and greets everyone who enters and sees that their requests are met. I have never been able to look at her beauty without blushing red lights of embarrassment. She will laugh at me and look even more beautiful. She loads me with books for my requests and I go to sit in a room with a sparkling brook that flows by numerous comfortable chairs with soft lights for reading. Music plays everywhere.

The books in the library open in scenes designed to exemplify what you are studying. The wisdom books are my favorites. The participants act and speak, and events unfold in front of your eyes through entire centuries on Earth in order to demonstrate the effects of small acts of wisdom at critical moments in time. Long sessions can be spent in the library immersed in these inquiries. The books are sensitive to your every thought and idea, and the pages open and move through events accordingly. There are many books by our Instructor there and they are true treasures of insight. When opened they fill the entire room with sound and light that alone is awesome. The wisdom she discerns is beyond comprehension, and yet it is always so simple and loving and true.

∞

VI

The color of mercy is the white of forgiveness. Colors in Heaven are only acquired by acquiring God's attributes. Each of God's attributes carries a particular color, and each shade and variation of that attribute carries a corresponding shade and variation of the primary color. Our Instructor can hold a power of blinding white mercy that makes all else look gray. These are some of my favorite sessions. We work at mercy by seeking to meld with her color. We flex our white colors the way a body builder would work a muscle, and afterwards we thrill to see that our whiteness has increased. The way we flex our white color is by accepting God's mercy into our souls. God's mercy is limitless, and ultimately, you can only accept so much at a time. You have to stop and grow. Like all of God's attributes, mercy must be asked for and accepted before it can be given. When our Instructor feels that we are ready, we begin to study our particular mission to Earth. We have closed sessions with our Instructor and when we understand all that we have seen, and we are keenly tuned to the colors we are seeking to influence on Earth, we join hands and descend with our Instructor into the Light of Creation.

Mercy missions are my highest thrill in coming to Earth. No matter how dark the situation we arrive at, the pure white of our Instructor's light removes any doubts of failure. Our Instructor gives off God's mercy in light so pure, so white and so bright it removes all the dark ravages of diseased thoughts and feelings of failure that we find before us, all the fear blown clutter of disaster melts away under that redeeming light. It is all I can do to hold my own light steady. I tend to weep. When we arrive back in Heaven we all weep, and smile, because we know we have succeeded. The sense of weeping and exhilaration is difficult to convey. After these missions we all need rest, even our Instructor. Our colors are drained. God's mercy is unlimited, ours is not. Shedding pure white light in such intensity is an eventual strain. Our Instructor will disappear into her white stone house and we will not see her for long periods. Most of us go to her stables. Resting in Heaven may sound redundant, but everyone's work eventually needs respite, and like everything else here, rest is special.

Our Instructor is a master of horses and she keeps next to her house enormous stables with some of the finest horses in Heaven. One of the highest thrills in Heaven for me, and for most of those I work with, is to ride those horses. We go to her stables like children laughing and giggling and running off to play. The horses are muscled, sleek, intelligent, and as eager as we are to ride off as has never been imagined on Earth. There are hills and rolling country and crystal lakes to swim nearby, to travel through for periods of time which have no measure. We do not think of Earth at these times. We do not think of anything. We refresh.

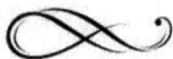

VII

The color of love permeates all that is. There are some who say that love is not an attribute of God at all, but that God is love. These are things best discussed in the Council of the Wise in Heaven. I do not know the answer, or if there is an answer to know. Love is red, I do know, bright red. But love, unlike mercy is measured by degrees of intense heat. It does not matter how much mercy is poured out in a given situation, no one can be adversely affected by too much mercy. Love, however, can be lethal, and love must always on Earth be tempered with mercy and wisdom. There is no such thing as showing up on Earth with God's pure love in mind. It would burn up the situation we have come to heal.

Love alone is hot, too hot, and this is why, so it is said in higher places, we can never finally approach God's presence. God's love is ever too hot, and though we can come close, we can never come into the actual presence of God, or we will burn up, literally. I do not know. I have never tried to approach God in such a fashion. I would not dare. Pure love, I do know, is difficult to hold and study. It does get hot. Our Instructor's love can blaze so hot, many of us will collapse in the room during sessions. Her love is not to be confused with mercy. In pure form, love is ferocious and never afraid, and our Instructor is fearless. Her love rises like a giant red rage and she will charge alone if need be into any adversity. Her love knows no obstacles. It can be truly frightening to behold at first, and it can take some getting used to. Our sessions of love are always tempered with wisdom, mercy and shades and variations of love. Kindness is a shade of love with a cooler temperature, and kindness itself has many shades and degrees. Our Instructor knows how lethal love can be, and her tender kindness is like a soothing balm. Loving too much is a common ailment in Heaven, and care is taken to always use love wisely. Love wants immediately to be shared, and often it cannot be shared. Sharing intense degrees of love unwisely can be harmful.

Our missions of love always entail great patience. We must hold a delicate balance of wisdom, mercy and love for long periods. The goal is to maintain the same color throughout. This involves all of us knowing one another well, and matching and compensating for each others pulsating colors. Our colors, if you were to see them in slow motion, always pulse, as does all of life. All of life has a pulse and rhythm, nothing is static and constant. We must stay tuned to one another. There are always twelve of us on every mission, including our Instructor. It is an important number, though there is much I do not know about the number, our number makes a unison. If there are less than twelve, the mission will fail. Why, I do not know, but if there are only eleven available, we cannot descend into the Light of Creation. We are all twelve here now and our colors are consistent.

VIII

Love is the power and heat of all Creation. The power generated from this heat is what drives all of Creation. Nothing moves in Creation except by the heat and power of God's love, and everything moves. Nothing is without movement in all of Creation. Love pervades every movement, every breath that is taken in every molecule and aspect of Creation. The heat of all Creation cannot be measured, and this immeasurable heat of all Creation is contained in every single part of Creation no matter how small.

The heat of love that moves all of Creation, also binds all of Creation. Love is the great connector and binding substance in every corner of Creation. It connects us all, on Heaven and on Earth. We are bound to our Instructor by her great love. It is a bond that will never release us. Our Instructor is bound by God's love and that love is eternal. She is able to travel the closest to God, and absorb love of a measure and degree that would disintegrate all of us. She shares that love with us, and with all the Earth. Our Instructor's mission and passionate care is the Earth. She was present when the Earth was conceived. Many were placed in charge of the Earth, and she was one of them. She will remain forever.

Our missions into the Light of Creation, our souls ablaze in God's love, are to heal shattered hearts, and they are also missions of connection. We come to Earth to heal love's wounds and to reconnect feelings of loss and loneliness. No one is alone in

all of Creation. All are loved equally.
The very fact that you breathe proves
it. No breath is drawn but for the power
of love. We are all here with you and
loving you now.

IX

    Love binds all of Creation. There is a complete oneness in love that is ever inclusive. Love emanates from only one source and flows in only one direction. But love can get blocked and shunted off in circular directions and many colors can be adversely affected. This can be easily seen in the colors because colors never stay still, they flow. A blocked color is obvious immediately, especially bright red. Unfortunately, things are seldom done immediately. Colors get distorted and no longer pure. The beauty of red can become quickly distorted and cold and totally unrecognizable. These are the kinds of problems our Instructor and others like her study as they examine the Earth. When a decision of action is reached, our Instructor calls us together for a silent prayer for love in our hearts and wisdom in our minds. We usually begin by studying the scenes she displays for us in her pool of bright water.

When we arrive on Earth on a mission of love, the practical aspect of what we are doing is seeking to open lines of connection among twelve individuals all at the same moment on the Earth. Our purpose is to allow the color of love to flow more freely in all the multiples of colors that emanate from twelve individuals on the Earth. We do not send out the pure raging love of God, though in our sessions with our Instructor this is in fact what we do. My particular mission on Earth can be as simple as seeking to influence someone to make a call to another person. I might do this by gently sending out thoughts of good memories of a particular person or event. We take up twelve such places on Earth which can be close by, or long distances apart on the planet, and we all act at precisely the same moment in time. All of our tasks can be equally small, but all of them are equally critical. These missions take the most planning in closed sessions with our Instructor. There are many set scenes, which must be carefully reviewed with her, and more possibilities of future outcome than I can ever remember. We must know a great deal about the individual we are seeking to influence and we study their colors carefully. There are so many different and subtle colors we must influence by delicately and patiently emitting a particular shade of love under the right amount of wisdom to a particular individual. No matter how far apart we are on the Earth, we can all see one another well, and we are never out of our Instructor's vision.

In the study sessions on love with our Instructor before a mission of love, we see how connected every individual is to every other individual on Earth, and how every affliction in love can be equally connected to every individual on Earth. The mathematical possibilities of twelve amongst the billions on Earth in terms of the many variations in colors, is awesome in itself. This is the kind of knowledge our Instructor carries with her. She knows the exact color result we are seeking. When she sees that result achieved, our mission is over and we return home to Heaven. The results seen in the pool of bright water can be awesome in their beauty of flowing colors. When love is released, the torrent of love's flow over the Earth is beauty itself. I love to watch the flow of love. The colors it incites everywhere it flows are mesmerizing, and after a mission of love we always stand awestruck the longest in the cool of the evenings at our Instructor's pool of bright water.

X

Love is Power in Heaven, and our Instructor holds Power in Heaven because she holds more of God's love inside of her than can be even imagined. Our Instructor is the ultimate power and authority for this entire section of Heaven. She rules here because her great love binds all who dwell here. I have not traveled over much of this section of Heaven, and I have not been to other parts of Heaven, but I know that this small section of Heaven holds more cities of immense numbers of souls than I can count. All who dwell here love our Instructor with a devoted loyalty and steadfastness that cannot be known on Earth, yet, relatively few in Heaven have ever seen her. It is an immense honor that I am here at the center of her work and actually living in her household. Heaven for the most part rules itself. Earth is our Instructor's primary concern and she seldom visits in Heaven. Only in a very rare instance does our Instructor intercede in our section of Heaven. There are often visits to our Instructor for consultation and wisdom from all over Heaven, not only from our section. She has many concerns in Heaven, but Earth is her primary concern.

Our Instructor's love of the Earth is of fierceness as to make rocks melt and evaporate. She takes our work very seriously. Our trips to the Earth are chosen with such care and great prayer as only she can incite. We are totally dedicated to her every command and focused at all times on the tasks she has given us. We have our failures. Our Instructor takes them very hard. Her weeping in great sorrow is difficult to witness. All Heaven can hear her, and all stand still, heads bowed, no one can move, it is difficult to breathe.

XI

Our Instructor is a Keeper of the Light of Creation. She is one of its many Guardians. When I say that we go from Heaven to the Earth by holding the hands of our Instructor, we do not go to the Earth as you might imagine it. We descend with her into God's mysterious Light of Creation, and this may become difficult for you to imagine. There is an actual place inside that great Light of Creation where you are now residing which you call Earth. You may imagine that you are now sitting at a table on solid ground. However, you are in fact sitting in the middle of a mysterious blazing light, caused in no small part by the bright light of your own bright soul. All of Creation is being forged into existence before your very eyes, could you only see it. The concept you carry of the on going moment-by-moment sequence of events of life on Earth is a necessary illusion for your development. Each moment of time on Earth, however, is not a continuation of the last moment of time on Earth, but a completely new recreation of every thing that is in every moment of time on Earth. Every moment is a completely new moment in the ultimate sense. There was never one singular moment in time where everything was brought into creation and life began to move forward. The Light of Creation was not created in time, and it is not moving forward, it is pulsing in place. It has no time. It is God's light, and it is eternal. Every moment of time is a new singular moment, a complete recreation of the Universe. The Light given off by this divine process is the

Light of Creation. It is because of this fact that we have the unique opportunity, in each new pulsating moment that occurs in the Light of Creation, to infuse that moment with new meaning and color. When we infuse the moment with Heavenly colors, we pulse to the rhythm of the Light of Creation, the mysterious rhythm of God. Our Instructor is our ultimate leader in this regard, for she is the conductor, she knows the rhythm and the beat of God's Creation, and she teaches it to us.

I have not given you all the Heavenly titles of our Instructor at her behest. She has not wanted to distract you before she has instructed you. On Earth, many have called these beings Archangels. She is that, and much more in Heaven. They were God's firsts, even before Heaven. They were placed there for us, to see to the forging of our souls in the great fire of God's love, the love that fires the Light of Creation. These great beings were there to witness the firing light of the Light of Creation from out of the depths of God's great Soul, they were

78

charged with its eternal care, they will never leave their posts, and their vigilance is eternal.

XII

The small message from our Instructor is that Heaven is real, more real than Earth. She has asked me to leave you with some of my impressions of Heaven, and I have done my best. Her other short message is that God cares about the Earth. The chosen firsts in Heaven have been left eternally in charge of the Earth with instructions to never leave. Their care of the Earth is measured by the great power of love they possess, for they, too, have free will. They spend all of their enormous power and unimaginable efforts on the Earth. We are their constant concern, Earth is never alone. Heaven would be abandoned before Earth would be left. The Earth is loved with a divine and eternal focus of tender loving concern, and all on Earth who have ever imagined themselves lost, have never been so and never will be, no one is ever left, the care is eternal. Our Instructor is not a Messenger to the Earth in her work. God has gone to great lengths to place Messengers on the Earth, and these notes are meant only as encouragement. May you be always loving, merciful and wise; may you never feel alone and uncared for; may we meet in Heaven.

www.ingramcontent.com/pod-product-compliance
Lightning Source LLC
Chambersburg PA
CBHW060035050426
42448CB00012B/3020